Praise for *Bathed in Moc*

As it moves back and forth over time, *Bathed in Moonlight* explores the ambiguity of what is lost and what is gained in poetry. While Vassiliki Rapti's poems certainly engage with the voices of her native Greek tradition, they would also seem to be in dialogue with poetries beyond the borders of the Western world. She tends to locate individual experience in the collective. And so, with intense lyricism and transformative, vivid expression, each poem creates its own separate world of emotional strength. These poems are fluent, vibrant, reflective, sensitive, open and brilliantly sensory. They reflect Rapti's wonder at the world, the cyclic nature of life and language. Her voice spins, floats, and whirls from spiral shells, floating lakes, the ever vigilant moon and calls through fragments of memory, the depths of the underground and the unspoken that hides between each line.

—Gonca Özmen

Vassiliki Rapti's luminous, capacious poems are journeys arising from hope and fears; aching and searching, they seek kinship and reconciliation with nature which is the true home for the restless, solitary self. Sensuous yet balanced, sparse yet containing multitudes, *Bathed in Moonlight* illuminates the life of the mind where remembrance and unbridled thoughts run together, where human yearnings are an enduring life force, where words, written from the innermost place resonate and affirm the power of poetry. This marvelous collection of poems is a balm in our fractured and chaotic time.

—Pui Ying Wong, author of *The Feast*

Bathed in Moonlight

Vassiliki Rapti

Translated from the Greek by Peter Bottéas

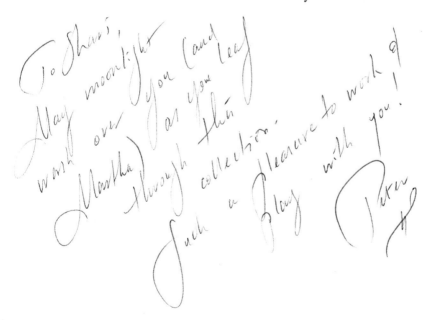

To Sharri,
May moonlight wash over you (and leaf
Martha) as you through this collection.
Such a pleasure to work of
Such a Blessy with you!
Peter

Červená Barva Press
Somerville, Massachusetts

Greek edition, *Η λεπταίσθητη Λαίδη μου*, published by Εκδόσεις Μελάνι [Ekdóseis Meláni], Athens 2021

Translated with permission from Εκδόσεις Μελάνι.

English version re-sequenced and augmented with 15 additional poems.

Červená Barva Press
P.O. Box 440357
W. Somerville, MA 02144-3222

www.cervenabarvapress.com

Bookstore: www.thelostbookshelf.com

Cover Art: *Εκεί που κοιμάται το φεγγάρι* [*Where the Moon Sleeps*], Hara Papatheodorou

Cover Design: William J. Kelle

ISBN: 978-1-950063-76-5

Library of Congress Control Number: 2023930900

ACKNOWLEDGMENTS

Deep gratitude to my English and Greek publishers, Gloria Mindock of Červená Barva Press and Popi Gana of Melani Publications, respectively, and of course, to my translator and dear friend, Peter Bottéas, who showed such love and dedication to this work!

Warmest thanks also to Hara Papatheodorou, who graciously offered her exquisite artwork for the book cover, and deep appreciation to the poets who generously offered their critiques: George Kalogeris, Pu Ying Wong, and Gonca Özmen.

It would be an omission not to acknowledge the editors of the following journals who granted us permission to include in this collection the poems that first appeared in their publications: Catherine Strisik of *Taos Journal of International Poetry & Art*, Iossif Ventura of *Poeticanet*, Stratos Fountoulis of *Stáchtes*, Thodoris Kintapoglou and Zoe Samara of *Theuth*, Rodica Draginescu and Carmen-Francesca Banciu of *Levure littéraire*, and Nestoras Poulakos and Stratos Prousalis of *Vakxikon.gr*.

Heartfelt thanks also to the members of *Citizen* TALES Commons for their constant encouragement, and especially to our supportive friends, Maria Kakavas, Vladimir Bošković, Julia Dubnoff, Jodie Cohen-Tanugi, Ivaana Muse, Despina Kaïtatzi-Choulioumi, Chloe Koutsoubeli, Vinia Tsopelas, Theodouli Alexiadou, and Stelios Karagiannis, as well as to my sisters, Evangelia, Mara, Eleni, and Ioulia, to my husband, Andreas Triantafyllou, and to our daughter, Katerina-Maria, to whom this book is dedicated.

TABLE OF CONTENTS

TRANSLATOR'S FOREWORD

Moon in a Double or Single Orbit?   3
Pathway   4
On a Boat Crossing Lake Hsieh   5
Dwelling   6
My Very Fine Lady   7
What is she to you?   8
Directions   9
Dunes   10
Enigma   11
Waves of Love   12
Late at Night   13
Miraculous!   14
Fragments   15
Finally   16
Arriving Anew   17
The Bride's Pursuit of Joy   18
Alone for so Long?   19
The Hum of the Earth   20
More Than Merely a Hum   21
Perpetual Perseverance   22
Vibrant Illusion   23
Breath Stopped Short   24
In the Footsteps of Esther Bessalel   25
The Canyons' Lament   26
On the Women Who Nurtured You   27
How could you leave the dancer to dance alone?   28
Five Haiku   29
Mind Splashes   30
True Pruning   31
Gaze from the Depths   32
Lilith the Muse   33
Years of Oblivion   34
Which Pathway?   35
Desolation   36
Spiral Shell   37

Stillness   38
Deep Night   39
Freedom   40
Anthems in the Garden of the Wild Pears   41
The Eye of Springtime   42
Elephant Moon   43
Song of Seashells   44
Dancing with Pan   45
Sipping Moondrops   46
Modern Light   47
The Body of the Moon   48

NOTES

ABOUT THE AUTHOR

ABOUT THE TRANSLATOR

For Katerina-Maria,
light of my life.

TRANSLATOR'S FOREWORD

Vassiliki Rapti´s poems are like delicate watercolors painted with a
fine brush, in hues of the seasons, the sea, and the night illumined
by the moon. They're diaphanous hues that give glimmers of an
inner world: warm, deep, subterranean pools of feeling, reflecting
yearning that might not otherwise see the light.

Working on these poems was a meditative experience and, at times,
a linguistic jigsaw puzzle—a challenge that stretched this translator
both intellectually and emotionally. Though Vassiliki's primary
medium of expression is Greek, a half-dozen of these poems came
to her spontaneously in preliminary English iterations, which
eventually gave rise to her masterful Greek versions. In some cases,
the poems morphed significantly as they found their way back to
her innermost voice, in her most intimate lexicon. My task involved
hearing her authentic voice through her English prototypes and, at
the same time, culling the nuggets of shimmering metals from her
Greek renditions, spinning them together in a translational
centrifuge and seeing what emerged. It is my hope that this English
collection will touch readers outside of Greece as profoundly as the
original version has moved Greek readers.

Peter Bottéas
Marblehead, Massachusetts

Bathed in Moonlight

Moon in a Double or Single Orbit?

Like a drawing
that takes you
back to your roots
or
to a pathway
opposite far-away clouds
summoning
the relentless resonance
of a solitary heart
to a fathomless
ineffable silver glow

The orbit of the moon as it once was

Pathway

To one side
fractured sunbeams scatter
after the downpour
Eyes half-open
are dazzled
by luminous loveliness
Peach blossoms
like flickering lanterns
covered in dewdrops
illumine
the lotus within

On a Boat Crossing Lake Hsieh

At dusk
on the western shore of Lake Hsieh
a festive blanket of silk—
grapevines, honeysuckle and lotus blossoms—
await pretty girls
shrouded in incense
and reticent smiles
like sages conquering grief
over a world crafted from dust
tying knots
climbing
—though not as in times past—
the gate of prehistoric mystery
where each ridge
senses the dappling light of twilight

Dwelling

for CK

Round and full
chaste love
would flow over you
enticing
the moments
we might share

My Very Fine Lady

for Jodie

As I set off to war
your gaze
fractures the silence
of millennia
This manner of yours
nests in my mind
Your eyes:
my entire world

What is she to you?

Balance
Truth
A quest
One you're afraid of
Someone you live deep inside of
Rollicking on the ground
A wellspring of light
A whip raging in the wind?

Directions

for JD

A desolate wind blows
on Plum Island
When you left, were the beach plums in bloom?
Was it then that people radiated with joy?
When our home still treasured
love and laughter?

That wisp of a lady
you once courted
never left
She is still there maneuvering the halyard
of the raging wind
that will bring you back

Dunes

The years
swirled
spinning
sea sand
into cliffs

You see,
they never let
the cypress trees
stand in their way

The moonlit night
secretly smiled
through all those years

Enigma

Cliffs, cascades, creeks, birds
Floating life
on dazzling-clear days
weaving blossoms of longing
Pear blossoms
inhaling mists
out of gossamer floss
Sacred adoration

Waves of Love

Asleep
early
on a
frozen
orchid
a northerly
dragonfly glowing
suddenly trapped
in an empty bookcase
silver pillars
of recollection
roused by
the glimmer of a
missing gemstone
lamenting
emerald waters
beckoning her to
limpid lyrics
that waken
searing waves
of love

Late at Night

We said our goodbyes
swirling
in a cyclone of stars
Drunk with love
we banished far
the mournful dawn

Miraculous!

Each day
the simple space between us
with a smile
shrinks the distance
magnifying our magnificence

Something miraculous to fathom!

Fragments

The ways of the world
elude you
Any way around it?
What if we changed
the map of the stars?
Wistful, ever wistful . . .

Finally

The snowflakes have finally fallen
on the grassy green and
the willows have reverently bowed
to the fate of Nature

And she
with the deepest of sighs
has finally bowed to
the innermost
primeval solitude

Arriving Anew

The flock is in its prime
as I gather firewood
and climb into your garments
Endless thoughts of you
swirl in radiant beams within me
The vision of your striking form
dark and deep, bittersweet
revisits me at last

The Bride's Pursuit of Joy

Pursuing unadulterated joy
she scatters the rays of the rainbow
tossing aside her lily-white gown and
rushing barefoot
into the crystalline meanders
of the waterfall

Alone for so Long?

Goddesses of the dance
fill the hall with grace
and a scent of cinnamon
inducting young maidens
into the rites of wedlock

The poet stealthily listens
behind the mauve orchids
and white peach blossoms
and through the keyhole
spies on the bride
heaving a sigh
beneath the limpid sheets

The Hum of the Earth

for Chloe

Tongue gone numb
wedding flowers gartering the thighs
the future chronicled
through gaps in History
in truncated breaths
in snipped petals
and in the hum of the Earth underfoot

More Than Merely a Hum

Buzzing hive
wondrously
crafting honeycombs
Pollen, sepals, blossoms
nectar
honey flowing
among the hive
harried
hum
homecoming!
The conductor and
the queen bee
in the dance
A million maiden drones
abuzz
in a sweet dither
conversing
with each other
as honey
is brought forth

Perpetual Perseverance

At dawn
omens of your birth
from the depths of the night
swayed on the steps of your dwelling
seeking simplicity
Tugging at you through
an unfamiliar gate
after ages in the mist
you were cast among myriad
multicolored peacocks
so that you might learn the skill
of perseverance
dragged out, freed after aeons
flung, whirling, whirling
into the embrace of the moon

Vibrant Illusion

Brooks
whispering
things
memories
that
come from
noble sentiments

Random thoughts
that suddenly take flight
become cinders
soaring high
in a vibrant illusion

Breath Stopped Short

From the depths of a silver screen
unbridled thoughts emerge
stumbling through the night
astride a horse
being torn into a thousand pieces
as it gallops through the sky

In the Footsteps of Esther Bessalel

A tribute to Nikos Engonopoulos

Why not make that splendor
of tranquil azure
all around heaven
small enough
to hold in our hands?

Knowing nothing
of the mystic pillars
of her radiant hair
a passion unfulfilled
takes root in his ferocious heart

Beyond borders
For good

The Canyons' Lament

Sailing southern seas
in the light of day
young women
of a certain race
murmur
"Why all this waste?"

Steeped they are
in ancient tales
accounts from the depths of time
those landscapes
and narrow canyons
where all things reside

On the Women Who Nurtured You

for Benny

I searched for you—
an invisible you
I had to unearth you
from the seabed,
from the bones
of the other women
who rocked you in tandem
I had to inhale again
your timeless scent
and feel again
how your arms embraced me,
how they trembled
as they crowned me
with the light of initiation
I had to lean by
your bed of marble
to listen to your pulsing heart,
which beats still
I had to . . .
once you'd left

How could you leave the dancer to dance alone?

You sent no dreams or fresh air into today
You, who sought nostalgia
in pebbles on the shore
you, who sensed the scent
of timeless narcissus on sky glass
you, who plucked
the very first violets of May
you, who frolicked among the pebbles
in all their stolen splendor

Hecuba of the Sea,
how did you fail to return
you, who led
the comely circle of maidens
and the lads who entered the illusion
on the edge of youth's folly?

Tell me, how could you leave the dancer to dance alone?

Five Haiku

I.
Palsied with grief
the silver body of the moon
wanders yet again

II.
Radiant ambition
dwells in grasses of springtime
spawned by deep rivers

III.
Boundless galaxy
over rugged surfaces
twice inscribed

IV.
Harmoniously
frozen spirits from beyond
enliven anew

V.
This desolate poem
is on a quest for incense
from the mountaintops

Mind Splashes

Sunset pool shadows
where a thousand water splashes
laugh unperturbed
if you follow them closely

Does remembrance matter
When deep underground?

True Pruning

Beauty surrounds
sound and mind
when pruning
blossoms
of excess
freeing
branches
of spirit

Impermanence
arises
when the moon
wanders

Gaze from the Depths

Limpid waters
of shimmering moonlight
wash over me

And from the distant
depths of the seabed
the blushing cheeks
of a sea maiden
reach upwards
leaving a gash
on my lips

Lilith the Muse

The torchlight on his fishing boat
wrings out the darkness
to assuage it tenderly
and illumine the void
at the seas's beckoning

And what if the wind rages?
In the echo of the night
it encounters its voice
on the very edge of silence
wrapped in something barely visible

With deft maneuvering
the tiny vessel
tenaciously lights
the submerged coral of
ginger-haired Lilith

Years of Oblivion

Rain pays a visit
a dark enigma
which, by chance, shrouds
the Anthropocene

Nurturing mist,
bring me your wine —
the wine of
the River Lethe,*
which knows how to snatch away
wreckage, screams, and sorrows

* Lethe, one of the five rivers of the underworld, the river of
unmindfulness.

Which Pathway?

The one that leads to Venus de Milo
the Mona Lisa
or the Winged Victory?

Paths intersect and
somehow trace chains of bacteria
in an imperceptible and delicate pattern of life
Crowds of solitary souls
sense the enigmatic smile
of Mona or the stormy rage of the ancient warrior

Relentlessly vying
for that intimate moment
of reconciliation with time past

Desolation

Desolation
on the far-off
silk road

I, too,
simmer
in the dark chamber
of a thousand years

My essence
follows birds taking flight
Forever desolate

Yet
I weave
the gateway
for their progeny

Spiral Shell

for Vladimir

Scorching day
An open sky
thrusts us
into its spiral shell

Infinite
strong
azure
harnessing
the southwest wind

To the right or to the left
we reach our outer limits
and then return
to the day of Promise

Stillness

Like my friend's
irrefutable
brilliance
a solitary bird vanishes
beneath a sky-river moon
blurring a ponderous
"Who am I?"
in the air

An orchard in full bloom
amidst aged trees
lazily beckons
the most exceptional honeybees
to drink its nectar
and release its sweetness

A solitary woman
eating apples
gazes at the mist
taking myriad shapes
over the cove
and ponders the kinship
of the distant clouds

Deep Night

Letters drawn
from desire
their forms no longer
of any significance
in the pursuit of glory
strewn
throughout the garden
like creeping vines

They become
grassy caresses
spawning moons
in a bittersweet wind,
dream-charmer

In just the same way
the morning sun
will bestow upon us
its eccentric rays
after the deep night

Freedom

Morning spreads across
the sorrows of distance
harnessing some
source of chance
Warmth has returned
my hair now white
The spring river
attends to the sky
and sparrows spy
my abundance
The boundless lake
is ready to swallow me
And set me free

Anthems in the Garden of the Wild Pears

Twilight in the orchard of wild pears
Delight in climbing the trees

The outstretched branches
like shepherds' pipes
intone impassioned tunes
marrying heaven and Earth

The serpentine brain
takes the stage
triumphantly

The Eye of Springtime

Ancient books
in God's cookery
open
the eye of springtime

This year
it visited the landscape early
translucent waters, persimmon blossoms, bamboo shoots
served on a most earthly
platter of vines

In the ever-deepening night
the birds of the sky
projected on screens
presage the places that will blossom

Elephant Moon

I sing
of the fragrant waters
beneath the veils
and the tugboats of hopes and fears

Through an ethereal gateway
the light carries an echo
of a vernal breeze
from very far away

My head in a dream
weaves waterfalls, hills and knolls
from strands of hair, nests
and spider webs

At night
the underground streams
have diaphanous demands

In a mirror reflection
a goblet of ruby-red wine
seeps into the bones
of the elephant moon

Song of Seashells

Seashells, hands, fingers, and fingernails
libations of mermen
offered for the souls
of unseen sailors
in the depths of the sea

Drummers of the deep
raise your tridents
and disquiet the waves
Amplify the cacophony
that carries on in the ocean's abyss

Dancing with Pan

A woman alone
beside a fishing net
left by a river lad
counts the birds
taking flight from the shore
As she breathes the scent
of wildflowers carried in the wind
from the magnolia grove
she beckons Pan
into a whirling dance

Sipping Moondrops

Alone
late
at night
as
my dream
wanes
it spies
a
solitary
bird
straying
as it
drinks in
moondrops

Modern Light

You wear it
like a lantern
on your body

Your own light
diaphanous
living matter

Outwardly reflecting
inward channels
of hope

Transforming
the sun's light
into an enveloping basin

There
nature is shaped afresh
and life renewed

The Body of the Moon

In a deep lament
the body of the moon
journeys anew

Exuberant light
of deep rivers
poses on spring grasses

The endless galaxy
makes an abrupt appearance
doubly impressed

Gelid spirits
harmoniously
come back to life

Incense from mountain heights
beckons
in a solitary refrain

NOTES

The earliest iterations of "Dwelling," "My Very Fine Lady," "Directions," "Dunes," "Enigma," and "In the Footsteps of Esther Bessalel" first emerged in English and were later adapted by the author into Greek, with some modifications in structure and content, and subsequently recast in English by the translator of this volume. "Freedom," "Five Haiku," and "Mind Splashes" were written by the author in preliminary English versions and reworked by the translator.

The Greek versions of the poems "Dwelling," "Fragments," "Late at Night," and "In the Footsteps of Esther Bessalel" were first published in the electronic periodical Στάχτες [*Stáchtes*] on December 24, 2015.

Preliminary versions of "Anthems in the Garden of the Wild Pears" and "My Very Fine Lady" appeared in *Taos Journal of International Poetry & Art*, Issue 8, 2016. The titles have been modified in this collection.

The Greek original of "The Hum of the Earth" appeared in the periodical Θευθ [*Theuth*], Issue 2, March 2016.

The Greek original of "The Body of the Moon" was published in the online periodical *Levure littéraire*, Issue 14, May/June/July 2018.

The Greek version of "Arriving Anew" appeared in the online periodical *Vakxikon.gr* (n.d.).

Preliminary versions of "More than Merely a Hum" and "Modern Light" were inspired by a workshop held in 2018 in Cambridge, Massachusetts, as part of an ongoing series, "Our Ludic Music," co-facilitated by Vassiliki Rapti and Ivaana Muse.

ABOUT THE TRANSLATOR

A native of Toronto, Canada, Peter Bottéas holds a Master's degree in Translation from the Université de Montréal and worked for many years as a translator, revisor, editor, and educator in French Canada. After a twenty-year detour as a psychotherapist in Boston, he recently returned to one of his first loves, literary translation, and is currently the primary translator of Greek Boston-based poet Vassiliki Rapti. The author and translator have done several poetry readings together in New York and Boston, as well as in on-line forums. He is a member of the multidisciplinary think-tank and creative forum *Citizen* TALES Commons and, along with Vassiliki, is co-host of the podcast series *Borders Unbound: Hellenic Poetry of the Diaspora and Beyond.* Peter is also an occasional voice-over artist, an infrequent poet, and an aficionado of French and Greek poetry set to music.

ABOUT THE AUTHOR

Vassiliki Rapti was born and raised in Greece, and studied Comparative Literature and Media in Greece, France, and the United States. She holds a Ph.D. in Comparative Literature with an Emphasis in Drama from Washington University in St. Louis, and is the author of several books, including *Ludics in Surrealist Theatre and Beyond* (Ashgate, 2013), the co-edited volume *Ludics: Play as Humanistic Inquiry* (Palgrave/MacMillan, 2021), and the bilingual poetry collection *Transitorium* (Somerset Hall Press, 2015). Her translation publications include Greek surrealist author Nanos Valaoritis, and her poetry and translations have been published in various international journals. She received a Parnassos Literary award in Greece in 1998.

Her poetry is fueled by surrealist imagery, a pursuit of playfulness in artistic expression, and a desire to capture wonderment in everyday life. She is Chair of the Ludics Seminar of the Mahindra Humanities Center at Harvard University, where she founded the Advanced Training in Greek Poetry Translation and Performance Workshop, and currently teaches World Literature and Digital Culture at Emerson College. She is the founding director of *Citizen* TALES* Commons, an international collective of scholars and artists.

The poetry collection that forms the core of this volume was published in Greek in Athens by Εκδόσεις Μελάνι in 2021. In November 2022, the Voice of Greece (Η Φωνή της Ελλάδας), the radio arm of the Hellenic Broadcasting Corporation (EPT), featured Vassiliki as its Poet of the Week, with twice daily readings of her poetry throughout the week.

*Translators, Artists, Ludics Learners, Explorers, and Storytellers

CPSIA information can be obtained
at www.ICGtesting.com
Printed in the USA
JSHW022321270423
40861JS00001B/154